ALL THINGS BEARS FOR KIDS

FILLED WITH PLENTY OF FACTS, PHOTOS, AND FUN TO LEARN ALL ABOUT BEARS

ANIMAL READS

THIS BOOK BELONGS TO...

_____

_____

WWW.ANIMALREADS.COM

CONTENTS

Welcome to the World of Bears	1
What are Bears?	5
What are the Different Types of Bears?	11
History of Bears	33
How do Bears Help the Environment?	37
Characteristics and Appearance	45
Life Cycle	53
Ten Fun Facts About Bears	59
Thank You!	73

WELCOME TO THE WORLD OF BEARS

Among the most adored and feared land animals on our planet, bears have a reputation for being fearless predators with superhero-level strength. In truth, they are extraordinary, intelligent, resourceful creatures that must continually navigate a wild world with ever-increasing human presence.

Scientists call bears an **indicator species** – this is an animal that is so smart, it can detect a healthy living space in an instant. If there are bears in a region *indicates* that the area is healthy and sustainable. If a region suddenly doesn't have any bears anymore, it's a clear sign that the area is in trouble. It could be polluted soil or other unhealthy factors.

In simple words, bears tell us if a specific place is doing fantastic or suffering. *Isn't that incredible!*

That's how important the existence of bears is on Earth.

These beautiful animals come in all shapes and sizes and are found in various regions of our world. They have unique sturdy bodies and incredible inner workings.

Did you know that female bears can just shut down their stomachs and kidneys during hibernation and still give birth to cubs?

This is one of many fascinating facts about bears we know you'll love discovering!

The best thing about bears is that they are known to love their family members the same way we do. Next time you hug your teddy bear, think of it as a beautiful, smart, and strong being that needs to be protected.

Are you ready to learn more about these amazing animals?

Let's get right to it!

WHAT ARE BEARS?

Bears are mammals under the *Ursidae* family. They are found in countries across North America, South America, Europe, and Asia.

Bears have large bodies, thick and layered fur, long snouts, non-retractable claws, and short tails.

Adult bears can vary greatly in size depending on the species. The smallest, the sun bear, grows to about 5 feet and weighs 150 pounds. The largest, on the other hand, the polar bear, grows to twice the length and about three times the weight.

Imagine a bear that is as heavy as four vending machines?! Now that's an impressive bear indeed.

Most bears can live for about 25 years in the wild and 50 if kept in captivity (*zoos and sanctuaries*). Unfortunately, human activity like tree logging and hunting means bears have a much harder time living in the wild. In captivity, their safety is guaranteed, but in the wild, things out of their control harm where they live – this is a sad fact.

Wouldn't it be marvelous if bears could be safe to live their best life in the wild, where they belong?

Yes, we think so too.

Bears are **omnivores**, which means they eat a variety of animals and plants. They use their super-strong noses to find their favorite foods — clovers, dandelions, blueberries, strawberries, and raspberries. For protein, they like rodents, fish, grasshoppers, and earthworms. Once in a while, they also feast on deer or moose.

That superhero-level strength is no myth! Bears are not only strong, but they are also incredibly fast. A grizzly bear, for example, can easily crush a bowling ball with its jaw (*you know, if it could get its mouth around it!*) and can run at an incredible speed of 40 miles an hour. Their sense of smell is said to be one million times better than humans', and their intelligence is off the charts. In fact, bears are famous for having the largest and most complex brains of all land animals of the same size.

Quite impressive, right? ... And it doesn't end there...

Bears are capable of detecting the ripest fruits on trees, use tools to play and hunt, are known to grieve deeply, and cry for weeks when separated. They are fierce protectors of their family – both adults and siblings will come to the aid of a cub in trouble. There is no doubt that bears are some of the most extraordinary animals on our planet!

WHAT DO YOU CALL A BEAR WITHOUT TEETH?

A gummy bear!

WHAT ARE THE DIFFERENT TYPES OF BEARS?

Today, there are eight species of bears in the world, each with its own distinct characteristics. All immensely beautiful, valuable, and irreplaceable.

Let's meet them, *shall we?*

NORTH AMERICAN BLACK BEAR (*URSUS AMERICANUS*)

The North American black bear is the most common bear type in North America. There are 800,000 of them on the continent, spread up all the way from the border with Canada in the north to the one with Mexico in the south. They mostly live in dense forests, where they forage for plants, fruits, and nuts.

These mammoth bears can grow to be over 650 pounds, but they climb, run, and swim really fast. Not nearly as large and strong as a grizzly, the black bear would nevertheless put up a tremendous fight with one if they were to ever meet. *Does this happen often, you ask?*

Luckily, because the two bear species prefer to live in different habitats, the two bear species don't get to meet often. And that's probably a good thing, considering they do live in many of the same regions of North America.

Given they are smaller, however, the North American black bear routinely climbs trees. Mama bears teach their cubs to climb high so they can get away from predators, which is a very smart tactic. Black bears are also incredible swimmers, and some have been recorded swimming many miles to catch fish and get away from threats.

Despite their name, North American black bears can also be brown, white, blond, cinnamon, and blue-gray.

"GRIZZLY" BROWN BEAR (*URSUS ARCTOS*)

When you think of big, wild bears, you probably have brown bears — **or grizzly bears** — in mind. You can tell them apart from other bear types because of their large head, shoulder hump, and long claws. Everything about a grizzly is designed for exceptional hunting – their enormous size, skill, speed, and ferocity make this one of the world's most respected predators.

A grizzly can grow up to a mind-boggling 6.5ft and weigh about 800 pounds (*adult male*) and 400 pounds (*adult female*).

Why grizzly? Well, because they are both adorably fuzzy with grey-ish tips on their fur and impressively fearsome. Experts believe the common opinion that grizzlies are aggressive to be an unfair exaggeration. This is, in fact, a perfectly peaceful animal. When threatened, however, it has an instinctive reaction to fight rather than flee.

This is one fearless giant who won't back down.

Sometimes, black bears are confused for brown bears, but the easiest way to tell them apart is by identifying the existence, or lack, of a grizzly's hump. The very obvious hump on the back of a grizzly is an astonishing powerhouse of muscles. Specifically, a muscle that drives the bear's front legs. These incredible front limbs can tear a tree trunk apart or dig through rocky terrain to build a nest.

A grizzly can chow down over 90 pounds of food in just a single day in the summer, a time of year when bears must overeat to build extra muscle – everything they need to survive harsh winters.

Like the North American black bear, brown bears can also be different colors that range from black to blond. You can find them in most national parks, like the Yellowstone National Park, the Glacier National Park, and the Katmai National Park.

Once upon a time, there used to be more than 50,000 grizzlies in North America, but due to aggressive hunting and deforestation, the animal almost went extinct. Luckily, the US introduced protective laws that safeguard endangered species, and the grizzly's numbers are slowly but surely, on the way up.

POLAR BEAR (*URSUS MARITIMUS*)

Polar bears are the biggest meat-eating land mammals in the world – and the largest of all the bear species. Adult males can grow up to 1,700 pounds, and adult females can reach 1,000 pounds.

The most famous residents of the Arctic Circle, in the far, far north of our planet, polar bears inhabit icy land masses in North America, northern Europe, and Russia. Although they spend most of their lives navigating the frigid northern seas, climbing ice floes in search of seals, their favorite source of food.

Since they spend a lot of time at sea, polar bears are classified as marine mammals. Unlike what many people think, polar bears are actually black. ***How can that be?!*** Well, you see, their skin is jet black, yet their fur is transparent, so it reflects the color of their icy habitat and makes them appear white.

This is only one of many traits that sets the polar bear apart from all other bear species.

Unlike their other furry friends, polar bears are carnivorous. They only eat meat like seals, beluga whales, and narwhals. If these marine animals are not available, polar bears will eat just about any nearby creature, from reindeer to rodents and even seabirds.

ASIATIC BLACK BEAR (*URSUS THIBETANUS*)

As their name suggests, Asiatic black bears are native to Asia and primarily found in India, Nepal, China, Taiwan, and Japan. Some people also call them moon bears because of the V-shaped crescent on their chests. They are much smaller than their northern cousins, with adult males only weighing up to 330 pounds.

The Asiatic Black Bear is a phenomenal tree climber and spends about half its adolescent life on trees. It is, in fact, the largest tree-dwelling creature in the world! When an Asian black bear becomes a little too heavy in later years, however, it will be inclined to spend more time on land rather than atop a tree. *That's probably a smart move.*

Unlike polar bears, the Asiatic black bear is not a picky eater, munching on various fruits, bees' nests, and insects.

This bear species is known to be the most **bipedal** – which means it can spend a longer time on two legs than all other bears. The longest walk on two legs that has ever been witnessed lasted an astonishing quarter of a mile!

ANDEAN BEAR (*TREMARCTOS ORNATUS*)

The beautiful Andean bear is the only species in South America. It is commonly known as the spectacled bear because of its unique face markings.

They have light rings around their eyes that look like eyeglasses against their black or dark brown fur, giving them their scientific name *tremarctos ornatus,* which means ***decorated bear.*** These markings usually extend all the way to their necks and chests. Scientists can easily identify each bear because markings are unique to each individual.

Andean bears like hanging out in trees, and they sometimes build leafy sheds where they sleep and feed. They may sound scary because of their shrill screeches and purring sounds, but they're actually very shy and tend to stay well away from humans.

GIANT PANDA BEAR
(*AILUROPODA MELANOLEUCA*)

Giant panda bears, usually just called pandas, are a type of bear native to China. They are one of the most recognizable animals in the world because of their appearance. They have a distinct black-and-white coat with black fur around their eyes, ears, noses, mouths, shoulders, and legs.

While other bears eat small animals and insects, pandas love bamboo! Pandas love these flowering plants so much that shoots and leaves make up 99% of their diet. Since bamboo isn't exactly overflowing with nutrition, the panda needs to spend about 16 hours per day eating their favorite food.

Amazingly, pandas have only recently been classified as bears. For many decades, debates ranged among experts because pandas also seemed to be similar to raccoons. Their exact animal family could not be determined until recently, so yes, finally, they have joined the awesome bear family!

Pandas may look cute — especially when they show off their handstands — **but you should never scare them!** Like other bears, they have strong jaws and teeth that can harm humans. Pandas can grow up to 5 feet in height and weigh about 220 pounds.

All up, China is home to about 2,600 pandas – most of which are still living in the wild in the country's luscious bamboo forests.

SUN BEAR (*HELARCTOS MALAYANUS*)

Sun bears are the smallest members of the bear family. The largest ones can only grow up to 4 feet and weigh just over 140 pounds. After the

Giant Panda, this is the rarest animal of its kind.

These small bears live in lowland forests in Southeast Asia. They get their name from the bib-shaped golden patch on their chest that legends say represents the rising sun. Like the spectacled bear, the sun bear's markings are also individual, so these creatures are easier to track in the wild.

Generally nocturnal, sun bears often climb trees to avoid humans. However, they can become aggressive when provoked, injured, or with cubs.

SLOTH BEAR (MELURSUS URSINUS)

The last of the eight main bear species is the sloth bear, an animal whose name definitely does not relay its true attributes. **This is no sloth!** In fact, the sloth bear is one of the fastest and most agile of all the bear species and was only named '*sloth*' due to its very long claws and teeth.

Their favorite foods are termites and ants, and because of this, they are missing their front teeth. This gap allows them to suckle their fave snacks right from the ground or off a tree trunk.

The sloth bear's most interesting trait is its incredible ability to defend itself. Sloth bears have evolved alongside tigers in Asia and have developed a natural aggression that makes it seem, well, **a little crazy**. Tigers will often leave the irritable sloth bear alone, thinking that it's probably not worth the hassle.

Pretty smart of them, we'd say!

Amazingly, the sloth is the only bear species that regularly carries its babies on its backs for several months. While all bear species are known to do this, occasionally, the sloth bear does it instinctively and full time for nine months. Of course, this allows the mother bear to keep her paws free to fight off predators (*like tigers!*), something it can effectively do even with two cubs on its back!

WHY DO PANDAS LOVE OLD MOVIES?

Because the films are black and white!

HISTORY OF BEARS

Modern bears went through an exciting evolution journey to become the animals we all know and love today. This journey began almost 40 million years ago. They evolved from small carnivorous mammals that showed characteristics of both dogs and bears, with stocky bodies but blunter teeth than other meat-eaters.

The first confirmed bears, called *Ursavus elmensis* or dawn bears, only roamed the earth about 20 million years ago. Like modern bears, they liked eating insects and plants.

Modern bears emerged over 5 million years ago. They were small at first, but some types grew quite big. These ancient creatures diversified and moved to various places across Europe, Asia, and North and South America.

During this time, the world was changing. Our ancestors saw drier landscapes, lower sea levels, and the formation of land bridges. This new world caused the bears to adapt to their environments, giving rise to the many types of bears living today.

WHAT DO YOU CALL A BEAR IN THE WINTER?

A brrrr!

HOW DO BEARS HELP THE ENVIRONMENT?

Some bear species throughout the world face extinction because of logging, agricultural expansion, and hunting activities. We should protect them at all costs because their presence is really good for the environment. These are some of the awesome things they do for their habitats:

FERTILIZE FORESTS

Over 20 years ago, a group of researchers studied how bears in British Columbia and Alaska affected plant growth in these regions.

Brown and black bears alike love salmon. When bears eat their favorite fish, they move them away from the waters and into the rainforests. Our bear friends do this because they don't want to attract other scavengers as they devour their meals. This process helps scatter protein-rich salmon remains throughout the land.

Scientists discovered that this helps trees and shrubs in nearby areas grow three times faster. They learned that the nitrogen found in the salmon remains does wonders for the plants! As a bonus, this procedure creates large woody trees along streams and improves the life span of salmon habitats.

MAINTAIN A BALANCED ECOSYSTEM

If not for bears, moose and deer habits could damage native vegetation. These animals often overeat plants from a single spot and trample them. These practices cause erosion and can further harm an ecosystem.

Thanks to bears, their prey doesn't stay put in one area for too long. While bears prefer eating plants and fruits most of the time, they scare other animals away and keep them on the move, so they don't eat up too many plants in one area.

DISPERSE SEEDS

What creatures do you imagine when you think of animals that disperse seeds? You probably think of birds, bees, and ants.

However, you shouldn't ignore bears' contributions in this area. Scientists say that mammals are huge helpers in spreading seeds.

Bears love eating fruits, from blackberries to apples to plums. According to a study, brown and black bears combined can spread over 200,000 seeds per hour per square kilometer as they walk around looking for food. Plus, bear droppings can hold tens of thousands of seeds!

BOOST ECONOMIC VALUE

Bears are charming creatures that naturally attract tourists and photographers. These people will pay a lot of money to spend time with bears. In fact, travel agencies create bear-watching activities for travelers! People from all around the globe would love to hang out with these beautiful beings —*from afar, of course.*

Our ancestors have always been fascinated with bears. You can read about these animals in myths, legends, and anecdotes. Today, people still can't get enough of them!

CHARACTERISTICS AND APPEARANCE

Bears are some of the most recognizable animals in the world. You can find them on signs for the World Wildlife Fund (WWF) or merchandise for the Memphis Grizzlies. If you look close enough, you can even find one on a Toblerone chocolate box!

As a group, bears generally have similar features. Bears have stocky, fur-covered bodies with short necks, legs, and tails. They have small eyes, round ears, large, pointed teeth, and curved claws that don't retract.

They also have thick teeth called *molars* for crushing plants. Bear teeth continuously grow throughout their lives, along with growth rings that help scientists determine their age. These rings are just like the rings in a tree!

Like humans, bears move on their heels. They shift their legs from both sides at the same time when they walk or run. Despite their size, they are pretty fast. At top speed, brown bears can sprint at up to 35 miles per hour, while polar bears can reach 25 miles per hour. They are also excellent climbers and swimmers, but they can't jump to save their lives!

During winter, when there isn't enough food for bears, some species use a very effective technique called *hibernation*. While this might surprise you, they don't sleep the whole time that they're hibernating. They simply don't eat or drink and rarely pee or poop. This allows them to stay in their dens, keeping their heartbeat, body temperature, metabolism, and breathing levels low.

Grizzly bears and black bears are master hibernators and can go 100 days without eating, drinking, peeing, or pooping!

HOW LONG DO BEARS LIVE?

Bears can live up to 25 years in the wild. First, their thick layers of fat and fur help them fight the cold and stay warm. Their long, curved claws help them dig and catch food. Their nails are sharp enough to pierce through fish, and they can really hurt any other animal.

When bears feel threatened, they fluff up their fur and stand on their strong hind legs to look bigger. They then bare their sharp teeth, pound their claws on the ground, and charge quickly at whatever makes them feel scared.

WHAT DO BEARS EAT?

Bears are omnivorous creatures, which means that they eat meat *and* plants. Polar bears are the only kinds of bears that are carnivores, which means that they only eat meat. This is because it's hard to find a lot of plants in their cold habitat.

In most cases, bears prefer berries, grass, grains, fish, birds, small mammals, and insects. Surprisingly, their diets consist mostly of non-meat food sources. However, if they smell human garbage close enough, they won't hesitate to look for pet food, honey, nuts, and other smelly foods.

WHAT DID THE BEAR SAY TO THEIR SIBLING?

Stop, you're being unBEARable!

LIFE CYCLE

Have you ever wondered how such a tiny baby bear can get so huge? Here's the life cycle of a bear, from babies to adults!

BREEDING

Between May to July, female bears mate with males. The males fight over the females, and they protect their mates as they fall into their winter sleep. Afterward, they stay in different territories and don't often come in contact until the next mating season.

PREGNANCY AND BIRTH

Bears often mate in June, but the babies don't really start to grow until around November. After seven months of pregnancy, mama bears give birth to one or two cubs between mid-January to early February. They can give birth to as many as five babies at a time!

Bears have some of the smallest babies compared to their mother's body size. For instance, newborn giant pandas only weigh about 100 grams, but full-grown adults can reach over 260 pounds. That's 1,200 times more than their cubs!

NEWBORN BEARS

Baby bears, called *cubs*, are born blind and covered with light hair. They can barely crawl at this age. When the world welcomes newborn bears, they are completely dependent on their mothers. Like human babies, they cry when they feel cold, hungry, or need to pee or poop.

Newborn cubs have mouths developed for sucking milk because that's all they can eat. Cubs don't stop nursing until they are about 18 months old, but they stay with their mothers until they reach about 30 months old.

YOUNG ADULTS

When bear cubs can fend for themselves, their mothers send them off into the world and start breeding again. Young adult bears have not reached their full height and weight yet, but they start eating larger prey. Between three to five years old, bears will become old enough to have their own babies.

FULL ADULTHOOD

By eight or ten years old, bears reach adulthood. At this point, they are fully capable of taking care of themselves, and they can live on their own.

Unlike other animals, bears are not territorial. Instead, they have home ranges where they share land, shelter, and food with other bears.

WHAT TYPE OF CEREAL DOES THE POLAR BEAR ALWAYS HAVE FOR BREAKFAST?

Ice Krispies!

TEN FUN FACTS ABOUT BEARS

#1: BEARS ARE SUPER SMART

Yogi claims to be smarter than the average bear, and bears are much more intelligent than we thought. Scientists believe that bears have large and complex brains that are super smart!

Are you wondering just how bright they are? Some species can remember food hotspots even after ten years. They know how to hide their tracks to avoid hunters, and they know how to hide their scents to surprise their prey.

Also, bears know numbers! Only the smartest animals in the world, like gorillas, chimpanzees, lemurs, dolphins, and elephants, can do this.

#2: BEARS HAVE THICK FUR

Bears are fluffy animals for sure, but they're not as big as they seem. **Their fur just makes them look huge!**

Polar bears have two layers of fur instead of one. The shorter layer protects them from weather changes, and the longer one prevents water from seeping into their skin.

Their winter fur can grow as long as five inches and reach almost 60 pounds! When bears feel threatened, they will puff up their fur to appear bigger than they are.

#3: BEARS HAVE FEELINGS, TOO!

Like people, bears can feel happiness and fear, and they can feel for other bears around them, too. Bears are social creatures. They play together and communicate using body language and sounds.

Mama bears may sometimes look scary because they are protective, strict, and attentive to their kids. When the young bears get separated from their moms, they can moan and cry for weeks.

Usually, they treat other animals like they would their fellow bears. Sadly, their playful demeanor might harm other kinds of animals since they are very physical beings and often bite and swat at one another.

#4: BEARS CAN WALK LIKE HUMANS

Bears often walk on all four feet, but they can also walk like people on their hind legs. They can do their human-like walk for short distances. However, they save this skill for special occasions, like when they need to see better, reach food, or scare hunters.

#5: BEARS ARE SUPER-FAST!

There's a myth about bears claiming they can't run downhill. It's absolutely not true. When bears pick up speed, they can run faster than horses! They can do it in all directions — uphill, downhill, or sideways.

Bears are not known to attack humans because they are not territorial creatures. However, if a bear ever chases you, it will undoubtedly outrun you. There's no point in running away from it.

Instead, help it recognize you as a friendly human. To do this, you should remain still, stand as tall as you can, slowly wave your arms, and talk loudly but calmly. Don't scream, as this will just scare the bear.

#6: PANDAS HAVE EXTRA BONES

While Po — you know, from Kung Fu Panda — loves steamed pork dumplings, real pandas prefer eating bamboo. They love it so much that they can spend up to 16 hours per day munching on 40 pounds of leaves, stems, and shoots.

Luckily, their bodies have adjusted to their food preferences. Their elongated, padded wrist bones on each front paw help them grip their favorite food. They don't act the same way thumbs do, and they're only useful for bamboo.

#7: SLOTH BEARS HAVE VACUUM LIPS

Experts also call sloth bears (melursus ursinus) *labiated bears* because of their unique mouths. They have specially developed muzzles that match their eating habits — lower lips and palates that suck up insects!

They love eating ants and termites. When they feel like eating insects, they wrap their lower lips around their noses and create vacuums with their snouts. They don't have upper teeth, so they can catch lots of critters in one go.

#8: POLAR BEARS ARE MARINE MAMMALS

Like walruses, sea otters, and seals, scientists classify polar bears as marine mammals because they need the ocean to survive. After all, they prefer hanging out on ice floes and eating sea creatures. For this reason, they are the only bears that fall under this category.

Their bodies have adapted to their icy habitats, with their webbed paws, an extra layer of fur, and versatile nostrils that close when they're underwater.

#9: BEARS MAKE THEIR OWN BEDS

No, we don't mean they fluff their pillows and straighten their sheets.

As long as there are food sources available, bears will stay outside. However, the moment the cold kicks in and there's nothing left to eat, they rest in dens that they prepare for the winter.

Bears usually use hollow trees, stumps, or ledges to create their nests. They strip bark from trees to use as bedding and fill these sheets with branches, leaves, and twigs. Pregnant bears typically go to bed first, followed by mother bears and their babies, and finally adult male bears.

#10: BEARS NEED YOUR HELP

Bears are massive, intelligent, and strong animals, but six kinds of bears are at risk of extinction. These are polar bears, Asian black bears, sun bears, sloth bears, Andean bears, and pandas.

The biggest cause of this is habitat loss. Because of pollution, wars, and wildlife trading, humans have destroyed a lot of the ecosystems where bears can thrive.

Check out the Raincoast Conservation Foundation, Andean Bear Project, and Polar Bears International to discover how you and your family can help these awesome animals.

THANK YOU FOR READING!

Thank you for reading our little book! We hope you had as much fun learning about bears as we did.

We'd like to remind you to be careful if you see these beautiful creatures. They are often shy and stay away from people, but they are also massive and super-fast. On the bright side, many people see bears without getting hurt every year. In fact, lightning strikes and bee stings are more likely to harm people than bear attacks.

If you want to keep learning about bears, ask your parents what your family can do to help endangered bears. Your family can check out the Raincoast Conservation Foundation, Andean Bear Project, or Polar Bears International to learn more about these awesome animals and what you can do to keep them around for the future.

THANK YOU!

Thank you for reading this book and for allowing us to share our love for bears with you!

If you've enjoyed this book, please let us know by leaving a rating and a brief review wherever you made your purchase! This helps us spread the word to other readers!

Thank you for your time, and have an awesome day!

For more information, please visit:

www.animalreads.com

PARTY

ANIMAL!

© Copyright 2022 - All rights reserved Admore Publishing

ISBN: 978-3-96772-113-3

ISBN: 978-3-96772-114-0

Animal Reads at www.animalreads.com

The content contained within this book may not be reproduced, duplicated or transmitted without direct written permission from the author or the publisher.

Under no circumstances will any blame or legal responsibility be held against the publisher, or author, for any damages, reparation, or monetary loss due to the information contained within this book. Either directly or indirectly.

Published by Admore Publishing: Gotenstraße, Berlin, Germany

www.admorepublishing.com

www.ingramcontent.com/pod-product-compliance
Lightning Source LLC
LaVergne TN
LVHW020141080526
838202LV00048B/3983